Awakening Of A Life Within

Her story is not a magic, but a life we live in

Aysha Nizamudeen

Made with ❤ on the BookLeaf Publishing Platform
www.bookleafpub.in
www.bookleafpub.com

Dedication

To those who feel alone,
who doubt their strength and potential,
remember, sometimes all it takes
is a gentle push.
You are not defined by your fears,
but by your courage to rise,
and within you lies the power
to achieve what you dream.

Preface

In a world where we often find ourselves grappling with self-doubt and feelings of isolation, this book serves as a beacon of hope and a journey toward self-improvement. Through the lens of fantasy, we explore the intricate trials faced by the characters, particularly Karen and Shawn, as they navigate their emotions and confront their fears. Each challenge they encounter is not merely a plot device but a reflection of the internal struggles we all face in our quest for growth and understanding.

The fantasy elements woven throughout the narrative are designed to entertain while also providing a deeper exploration of themes such as resilience, friendship, and the power of self-discovery. As Karen and Shawn embark on their journey through enchanted realms and face their innermost fears, readers are invited to reflect on their own experiences. The trials they undergo symbolize the obstacles we encounter in our daily lives, reminding us that confronting our fears is an essential step in achieving personal growth.

Ultimately, this book is dedicated to those who feel alone or believe they cannot achieve their dreams. It emphasizes that, with a gentle push and the right mindset, we can all embark on our own paths of self-discovery and improvement. Through the characters' journeys, I hope to inspire readers to embrace their challenges, recognize their strengths, and realize that they are never truly alone in their struggles. As you delve into this story, may you find encouragement and empowerment to pursue your own journey of self-improvement.

Acknowledgements

I would like to express my deepest gratitude to my parents, whose unwavering support and encouragement have been the backbone of my journey.
This book is a reflection of your sacrifices and the countless lessons you've imparted. I hope to make you proud as I continue to pursue my dreams, and I dedicate this work to you both, with all my love.

1. The restless heart

Karen lived in a small town near the mountains and seas,
Her life was perfect, or so it seemed to be.
With perfect parents, a perfect house, and perfect
friends,
But the pain she carries within her heart whispers no
ends.
Her hopelessness and fear drowned her wholly,
Wondering if there is something beyond her sight,
perhaps below the sea.
Her questions deepened when she sees the painting led
by the sun, who seemed to be free.
Her heart fluttered and her eyes wandered,
As she listened to the secrets of the mountains,
And the songs of the sea.
The calls she heard were breaking her cage,
Revealing mysteries beyond her wooden frame.
She lays in bed, visions as she rides with the wind,
Towards the sun, screaming her heart's voice within.
"Who are you out there, do you know me?
Can you feel me, can you set me free?"

But her dreams were just dreams that danced in the
night,
In reality, a distant star, beautiful yet elusive.
To leave a world with certain tomorrows,
Was deemed foolish to travel into the unknown.
So she lived a life beautiful and lovely,
But trapped in a cage, her wings clipped and buried.

....

2. Mysterious invitation

One crisp autumn morn,
As golden leaves shimmered bright,
Karen discovered an envelope,
Adorned with silver runes and sealed with a waxed star.
A crescent moon entwined.

A thousand tiny peaks rose on her skin,
As she touched the paper, a spark, an unknown feeling
within.
Her eyes followed the words that glowed,
As if starlight had kissed them, a magic unknown.

Dearest Karen,
We believe it's time to show your true embrace,
Beyond your wooden frame lies a realm where trees
speak with grace.
A moonlit path awaits as you wish to step forward,
Slowly, your journey will begin, within the enchanted
forest,
A new chapter shall be reborn.

With anticipation,
A Keeper of the Mysteries

Her heart raced as she read,
Her mind whirring, unable to unfold what the glowing
words had led.
"Non-sense is what it is", or so she thought,
The hidden realm too fantastical to be,
A dream too far away from her reality.
So she tucked it away, her doubts entwined.

3. A voice of confusion- By her

Maybe it's me who should talk to you,
For you don't know the way I feel or do.
The voices in my head, deep and sore,
The letter felt like an aid to my pain,
Yet still, the voices in my mind remain.
So hear me now, as my heart explains—

A magical place where I'd find who I am
Sounded too good to be true—
Or so I thought.
I pondered the letter, watching outside my wooden
frame,
The moon's light stretching to meet the sea.
And I heard it again—
The songs of the sea,
The whispers of the mountains.
I felt myself sink into their words,
Again...
Pulled deeper into their call.

And I thought—
What if I'm not imagining it?
What if their voices are real?
What if there truly is a world of magic?

4. Call of the unknown path

The following days began to change,
The once familiar roads now felt strange.
Old oak trees stood strong and tall,
Yet her eyes met them for the first time.
And then she saw the subtle, unmistakable sign,
Etched on the oak tree—a star emblem, crescent moon
entwined.
She stopped to see,
While no one cared to mind what it could be.

Since the incident, a week had passed,
She wandered the market, pushing past the mass.
A cloaked figure brushed her shoulder,
Sending a chilling shiver run down her spine.
The figure's brooch bore the same strange sign,
Before she could talk, he vanished within the line.

A few days later, she went to the library,
A familiar book she found with a waxen seal.
"Legends of the Hidden Realms," it spelled,

She read in whispers, revealing its secrets,
Of a mythical grove, a path illuminated by moonlight
itself,
That leads to a realm where one could discover their true
self.
She sought more answers at the desk,
But the librarian, surprised, and confessed-
It was the first time she had seen the book,
That now held Karen in its hook.
That night, the letter lay on her desk,
The moonlight made its emblem glow.
Karen stared, her mind swirling,
Questions, doubts—her thoughts whirling.
The signs, too compelling to ignore,
Yet too real to believe for sure.

"Could this all be mere coincidence?"
She closed her eyes, took a deep breath,
Sat up straight, needing to decide,
Her curiosity outweigh her fear,
The journey, once met with hesitation,
Now seemed a path of fascination.
Beckoning a promise of something more,
Something unreal, unknown, and unsure.
But she knew she had to take the leap,
To leave the familiar and see the deep.

5. The companion

Karen stood, heart racing, letter in her hand,
She'd made her choice to leave the known land.
But as her thoughts took form, the book began to shake,
A subtle tremor, then a quake.
Legends of Realms, the pages did glow,
As from within, a creature began to show.
With a burst of dust, and a glimmering gleam,
Appeared a sprite—more real than a dream
"Ah, finally! You're ready to go,
Took long enough to start this show!"
The creature grinned, arms crossed in play,
"Name's Thistle, by the way.
Yes, I'm real, no dream you see,
And I'm not just a guide—I'm your best friend to be."
Karen blinked, her thoughts a storm,
"A...gnome?" she asked, trying to conform.
"Gnome?!" Thistle scoffed with a scornful bite,
"I'm a sprite, thank you! Get it right!
Don't let my size fool your mind,
I'm the best guide you'll ever find."

Karen was shocked, but oddly so,
Not more surprised to watch him glow.
Yet, it made sense, she had to confess—
It was an enchanted forest, nonetheless.
Karen laughed, feeling light as air,
For the first time, her heart felt bare.
"Alright, Thistle, what comes next?"
Her voice, though calm, was still perplexed.
Thistle floated, perched with ease,
Leaning on her neck, whispering like the breeze.
"Now stop your thinking, start your stride,
The world awaits just outside.
You'll need a friend, someone to cheer,
To laugh with you, and calm your fear,
And when magical mishaps come your way,
I'll handle them, don't you dismay."
"Magical mishaps?" Karen's brow furrowed tight.
"You'll see," Thistle winked, eyes alight.
"But trust me, friend, it'll be grand,
Wilder than dreams, yet close at hand."
Karen smiled as the path lay ahead,
No longer filled with doubt or dread.
With her new friend, adventure felt right,
Into the unknown, beneath moon's silver light.

.

6. Stepping into the unknown

Karen stood at the edge of the forest,
feeling the weight of what was behind her.
A world so familiar, filled with routine and certainty,
but now there was something different—
a quiet pull from the unknown.
The letter, tucked safely in her pack,
promised more than she had ever known.

She hesitated, the fear of what lay ahead
mixing with the comfort of what she had left.
Thistle, perched on her shoulder,
broke the silence with a gentle voice.
"You're still unsure, I can see that.
But the unknown isn't as terrifying as it seems.
It's where the real adventure begins."

Karen exhaled, her breath heavy with doubt.
"I don't know if I'm ready for this," she admitted.
Thistle smiled, not with sympathy,

but with understanding.
"Few are ever truly ready.
But readiness isn't what matters—
it's the willingness to step forward."

The forest in front of her loomed large,
its shadows deep, its path unclear.
But for the first time,
Karen felt a flicker of something new.
It wasn't just fear—it was curiosity.
"What if the unknown holds something more?"
she thought, her heart beginning to shift.

With Thistle at her side,
Karen took her first step.
The forest felt alive,
not with danger,
but with possibilities.
The air around her was thick with stories untold,
and with every step, the past grew fainter,
the present more real.

She wasn't running from anything,
nor was she seeking to escape.
She was stepping into the unknown,
not to conquer it,
but to discover something within herself.

The journey wasn't about the destination,
but about the act of moving forward,
despite not knowing what came next.

Thistle, sensing her lingering doubt,
nudged her shoulder softly.
"You know," he said,
"You're already ahead of most.
Most people look at the unknown
and turn away, too afraid to step in.
But you? You're here, stepping forward.
That's the hardest part."

Karen paused at his words,
the weight of them sinking in.
She hadn't realized how much courage it took,
just to take that first step.
And somehow, that made her feel lighter,
as if the path ahead wasn't as daunting anymore.

"What now?" Karen asked quietly,
her voice blending with the wind.
Thistle, ever calm, ever steady,
replied, "Now, we walk.
We don't need to know everything right now.
We just need to keep moving."

As they ventured further into the unknown,
the moonlight began to filter through the trees,
casting soft beams that lit their path.
It felt as if the forest itself
was guiding them forward,
its mysteries unfolding in the gentle glow.

And so they did.
Into the unknown,
not with certainty,
but with the courage to see what might be waiting,
their way illuminated
by the soft light of the moon.

7. Into the unknown

The forest grew quiet,
As we stepped deeper,
Signs carved into the trees,
Old symbols, ancient and waiting.
Thistle smiled,
"We're almost there."
He motioned for me to sit.

"Close your eyes," he whispered,
"Think about what you wish to achieve,
In the next three months,
See it clearly, let it guide you."

I sat, breathing in the air,
The coolness of the ground beneath me,
I thought hard,
About all the things I wanted,
All the things I had yet to understand.
The world beneath me began to stir,
A tremor,

And then it opened.

I fell into the portal,
Colors swirling around me,
Bright, beautiful, yet blurred,
But the sadness of my past,
It stood out—
Clear as day,
Sharp as pain.

And then, I landed.
An upside-down world,
Yet somehow it felt the same.
The trees shimmered with gold,
Their leaves danced on the wind,
Singing softly,
A melody I had never known,
Yet always felt deep within.

I heard it—
The ocean,
It sang,
Just like I always knew it could.
I followed its voice,
Each wave a note,
Echoing my thoughts,
My dreams.

Then, from behind,
A whisper,
Soft, like a breeze,
Calling my name.
I turned,
But it was the mountains,
Their peaks leaning in,
Their whispers carried on the wind.
Everything I thought I imagined,
Was real in this world.

Thistle nudged me forward,
Guiding me along paths
That felt familiar yet strange,
The town, alive with colors,
The faces unfamiliar,
Yet filled with the same spark,
The same curiosity,
The same wonder.

Finally, we reached the old church,
A place long broken in my world,
But here it stood,
Whole and magnificent.
Thistle led me inside,
Where people sat, waiting,

And at the front,
A man dressed in robes,
Thistle pointed,
"That's the mentor, the one who will guide you now."

I looked around,
At the faces of those like me,
At the magic in the air,
At the life that breathed
Through every leaf, every stone.
This world,
This journey,
Had only just begun.

8. The mentor

The mentor's calm voice broke the hush,
"Welcome," he said, "tomorrow we'll begin this rush."
Introductions followed, names were shared,
Stories and hopes, vulnerabilities bared.
Karen asked, "Why was I chosen to be here?"
"In a world of acceptance, you sought more clear.
You wanted to change, to delve and to grow,
Potential we saw, that only we could show."
She took in the gravity, the mentor's words deep,
"The ones who leave will their memories keep?"
"No," he said, "they're erased from their past,
Replaced by clones to maintain balance at last."
With this weight on her mind, Karen prepared,
"To her new house, Thistle led, magic flared.
A door that opened with ease and grace,
Inside, enchantment filled every space.
A teapot that danced with a cheerful song,
Everything magical, nothing felt wrong.
She saw a classmate, a fleeting glance,
But her own new world held her in trance.

That night, she lay with thoughts running wild,
Wondering about the trials, as a curious child.
In this realm of wonder, where dreams blend and blur,
She readied her heart, her soul to stir.

9. The first trail

At dawn, I walked with heavy steps,
The path ahead unknown, unclear.
The shadows whispered, memories stirred,
And fear clung tight, but I drew near.
The mentor spoke, his voice was calm,
"Your trial is one of sight, not might.
To see beyond the fog of pain,
To find the hidden light."
Before me stood an ancient mirror,
A gateway to the depths inside.
I breathed deep, though fear was strong,
I knew I had to take this ride.
Through the glass, I fell in mist,
Where echoes of my past took shape.
The pain surged first, sharp and real,
While joy was distant, out of place.
I wandered through the shattered scenes,
The moments I'd tried to leave behind.
But faintly there, among the cracks,
Were fragments of love, of joy, entwined.

"You're already ahead," I heard Thistle say,
"In a world where most would turn away,
You've chosen to face what lies within,
To walk a path where others stray."
I reached for those faded memories,
Willed them clear, made them bright.
And as they grew, the pain fell back,
The burdens lightened, out of sight.
Each memory, a piece restored,
Fitted back with care, with grace.
The sorrow softened, lost its hold,
As joy reclaimed its rightful place.
At last, I saw a glowing door,
A way out of the maze of thought.
With steady steps, I crossed the line,
Into a world less fraught.
Back in the courtyard, I met his gaze,
The mentor saw what I had done.
"This is just the beginning," he said,
"But you've taken the first step, the hardest one."
I returned to streets alive with magic,
Where every stone seemed to hum.
The house I entered felt like home,
A place where I'd no longer run.
But I wasn't alone; Thistle was there,
And others, facing trials of their own.
I had passed the first of many tests,

But more than that, I'd grown.
That night, beneath the moon's soft glow,
I rested with a heart more clear.
The path ahead still winding, unknown,
But I was ready to face my fear.

10. A Hidden feeling

The morning light filtered through the trees,
Golden hues casting shadows on thoughts left unsaid.
Karen walked with a sense of accomplishment,
Yet unease clung to her like the mist in the air.
In this upside-down world, where magic danced,
She had passed the first trial, but the weight still clung,
A quiet echo of a challenge just begun.
She saw the others gathered, faces marked
With the same exhaustion she felt in her bones.
But two were missing—their absence a cold reminder,
That not all could bear the weight of their pain.
"Where are they?" she whispered to Thistle,
His usual cheer subdued, the answer heavy.
"They couldn't finish; their memories too much.
They're gone now, back to the lives they once knew."
Karen's heart ached for them,
For the struggle they couldn't overcome.
This journey wasn't just about magic,
But about facing the darkness within.
The mentor's voice cut through her thoughts,

A steady presence in a world of uncertainty.
"You've passed the first trial," he said,
"But remember, each step forward is a step inward."
Her gaze found Thomas, standing apart,
A boy with eyes that seemed to see beyond the surface.
Something in him mirrored her own fears,
A connection she didn't want, yet couldn't deny.
"Hi," she said, the word carrying more than just a
greeting.
He looked at her, his voice distant,
Like he was speaking from a place she couldn't reach.
"Yeah, I remember."
For a moment, they stood, two strangers
Bound by unspoken words and hidden scars.
Karen felt the tug of something deep,
But fear held her back,
A reminder of the past she wasn't ready to face.
"I should go," she said, the distance between them
Both a comfort and a sorrow.
"See you tomorrow?" she asked,
Knowing the second trial was already looming.
"Yeah, tomorrow," he replied,
His voice quiet, guarding the secrets within.
And as Karen turned away,
She knew this journey would challenge more
Than just her courage—it would test her heart.
And that frightened her most of all.

11. Second trail: the shifting maze

In the silence, the mentor spoke,
No hint, no guide, no helping hand,
Before them stretched the ancient maze,
A living, breathing, twisted land.
Dark stone walls rose high and tall,
Etched with symbols, faintly bright,
An entrance closed, a path revealed,
Their challenge hidden in the night.
Karen and Shawn, side by side,
Tread softly through the thorny way,
The vines that clawed, that cut, that bled,
Their patience tested, day by day.
They fought the thorns with every step,
But every move just pulled them in,
Till Karen whispered, "Not with force—
Let's try with care, let's move within."
They slowed their pace, their hearts in sync,
Each thorn a trial of mind and will,
They pushed ahead, their bodies worn,

But pushed they did, and all was still.
Through barren lands, the mirage gleamed,
An oasis of deceitful dreams,
But wise they were, they saw the truth,
And faced the chasm's silent screams.
The bridge, it swayed, with every breath,
Each step a dance with fear and doubt,
But forward still, they took the risk,
And found a strength they could not shout.
Their hearts were strong, their eyes ahead,
Through every crack, through every fall,
And when the bridge had turned to dust,
They stood as one, they stood so tall.
The fog rolled in, thick as despair,
A test of grit, a test of soul,
And though the path was dark and grim,
They knew they had to reach the goal.
Each step a war against the fog,
Each breath a fight to keep the flame,
But hand in hand, they pressed ahead,
And felt the warmth that bore no name.
The maze had shifted, twisted, torn,
But in its heart, they found their own,
For every thorn, for every crack,
Had built a bond, as strong as stone.

12. Second trail: maze's reckoning

The walls drew close, the earth did quake,
The maze, it sensed their beating hearts,
But fear was not to have its way,
They'd come too far to fall apart.
With shaking ground and closing walls,
The path ahead seemed all but lost,
But courage kept their feet in line,
No matter what the trial's cost.
Karen's voice cut through the din,
"We're almost there, we can't let go,"
Shawn nodded, eyes ablaze,
Their steps in sync, their spirits aglow.
The cracks beneath them spread like fire,
The maze, it roared with might and will,
But they would not be swallowed whole,
For they had climbed too many hills.
The exit loomed, so close, so far,
A sliver of hope in a sea of strife,
With one last leap, they made it through,

And held on tight to their thread of life.
The maze, defeated, closed its mouth,
But left its mark upon their souls,
For every trial that they had faced,
Had etched their hearts with unseen goals.
Breathless, they lay upon the ground,
Their bodies spent, their spirits light,
For though the trial had worn them down,
It forged a bond, deep as the night.
They knew not what the future held,
The maze's maze had shown no end,
But in each other, they had found,
A strength that no dark could bend.
Together, they would face the storm,
Together, they would climb the heights,
For in the maze, they found a truth—
That dreams are won through endless fights.
The mentor's voice, a distant call,
Announced the end of this first part,
But deep within, they knew full well,
The real trial was of the heart.
And so they rose, with purpose clear,
The second part was still unknown,
But with the bond that they had formed,
They knew they would not walk alone.

13. A voice of love- By him

I've known tough times all my life,
Where nothing comes without a fight,
A childhood carved from endless strife,
A battle from morning until night.

Each day, a struggle just to stand,
Pushing through with worn-out hands,
The weight of life, a heavy brand,
But never yielding to its demands.

Walls built high to keep the pain at bay,
A heart armored against the fray,
I told myself I'd be okay,
That loneliness was just my way.

But then I saw her, light and warm,
A beacon in the gathering storm,
Her kindness breaking through the norm,
Her presence gentle, yet so strong.

Karen, with her eyes so deep,
Pulled me from the shadows I'd keep,
Made me feel, though I'd dare not speak,
Of dreams that stirred from where they sleep.

In this world, so strange and torn,
She is the light of every dawn,
The one real thing that I lean on,
A truth, where all else feels forlorn.

With her, the fight is not so hard,
Her touch, a soothing, healing balm,
In her, I find my battle-scarred
Heart begins to mend, to calm.

For the first time, I feel not alone,
With Karen, the weight feels less like stone,
She makes me think of joys unknown,
Of happiness, once just a distant tone.

Yet still, I fear what could be lost,
For happiness comes at a cost,
But for her, I'd bear the frost,
To hold this warmth, no matter the cost.

She makes me want to try again,
To face the fear, to embrace the pain,

For in her light, I see the gain,
A life where love is not in vain.

Karen, you've become my guide,
Through the darkness where I'd hide,
With you, the shadows seem to slide,
And in your light, I find my stride.

But still, a part of me holds back,
Afraid to stray too far off track,
For with love, there's no turning back,
And my heart fears what it might lack.

Yet, with you, I think I'd dare,
To dream of love, to meet it there,
For in your gaze, I see a care
That makes me believe this life can be fair.

So here I stand, my heart laid bare,
Karen, in your light, I find my prayer,
To take this chance, to feel, to share,
A love that breaks through every despair.

14. The confession

In the fading light, they sit by the river,
Shawn feels his heart quiver,
"Karen," he breathes, his voice a soft call,
With words held tightly, he must reveal all.
"You've been my light in a life full of fight,
Through shadows and struggles, you make it feel right.
I've battled alone, but with you, I see,
A glimpse of the joy that could possibly be."
Her eyes meet his, a flicker of hope,
Yet doubt fills the space, a heavy, tightrope.
"Shawn," she whispers, her voice laced with fear,
"I care for you deeply, but I can't draw you near."
A weight on his heart, he feels the despair,
"Why pull away when I'm right here to share?"
But tears fill her eyes, she shakes her head slow,
"There's something inside me, a darkness I know."
"Whatever it is, we can face it as one,
You don't have to hide; let the shadows be done."
But she pulls back her hand, a barrier of pain,
"I can't let you in, I have too much to gain."

As twilight descends, silence wraps them tight,
The river flows gently, reflecting their plight.
He offers his friendship, a bond that won't fade,
Though love lingers close, it's a price to be paid.
"Thank you," she murmurs, sadness in her gaze,
In the stillness, they linger, lost in a maze.
He knows she's afraid, and so must he wait,
To stand by her side, through uncertainty's gate.
So, hand in hand, they walk back through night,
Two souls intertwined, in the absence of light.
Though walls may remain, and fears may still bind,
He'll cherish her heart, forever aligned.

15. The third trail

In the clearing, shadows gather, thick with secrets,
The air is heavy with unsaid fears,
The mentor steps forward, his gaze steady,
"Welcome to your final trial," he announces,
Words echo in the stillness, anticipation tinged with
dread.
"You will face what lies within," he continues,
"An obstacle shaped by your own emotions,
A labyrinth of doubt, a maze of heartache,
Where memories will rise, a reflection of you,
You must navigate alone, no companions in sight."
Each of us feels the weight of the journey,
Our hearts drum with uncertainty, a steady beat,
Karen's eyes flicker with shadows of the past,
Shawn stands firm, but I see the worry behind his gaze,
We're all here, yet alone, bracing for what's to come.
The mentor gestures, and the path unfolds,
A swirling mist beckons, whispers of lost dreams,
"Step inside," he urges, "embrace the unknown,
Face what you fear, unearth what you hide,

Only then will you find the way to your true self."
The ground shifts beneath our feet,
Each step pulls us deeper into our own stories,
As I glance back, their faces blur,
A reminder that this journey is ours alone,
And as the mist swallows me whole, I take a breath.

16. The shadow

As Karen stepped into the mist,
A shiver ran down her spine,
The air grew heavy, wrapping tight,
Obscuring all that she could find.
The world beneath her shifted low,
Familiar sights began to fade,
Echoes of thoughts whispered soft,
"Face what you fear," the mentor said.
The mist parted, revealing a path,
Darkened trees, twisted and bare,
Each step she took felt like a plunge,
Into memories she couldn't bear.
A vision flashed—a school hallway,
Younger self, alone in despair,
Laughter rang, a cruel taunt,
Friends with smiles, but hearts laid bare.
Betrayal sliced through her again,
Isolation, a familiar ache,
The weight of abandonment pressed down,
Filling her heart with sorrow's stake.

Then another scene, sunlit park,
Children's laughter echoed wide,
A boy approached, charm in his eyes,
For a moment, hope bloomed inside.
They shared dreams, secrets in the air,
But love turned to confusion fast,
He turned away, leaving her lost,
In a whirlwind of pain that would last.
Darkness crept in, a shroud of dread,
Memories twisted like a knife,
Every connection she had sought,
Had crumbled, left her void of life.
A shadow emerged from the mist,
A figure reflecting her fear,
Bearing her features, eyes cold as ice,
Its touch a reminder, heavy and near.
"Why seek connection?" it whispered low,
"When every touch leads to pain?
Each time you reach, you fall once more,
Into the abyss, alone to remain."
Heart racing, defiance took hold,
"No," she cried, "I'm more than my past,
I am not alone, I refuse this fate,
I will break free, I will outlast."
But the figure smiled, haunting and sly,
"Are you truly not alone?
Look at the shadows that follow you,

They're your companions, forever known."
With a roar of anguish, she fought back hard,
Memories swirling, a tempest inside,
The weight of betrayal and heartache pressed.

17. The heartbreak

Karen's memories unfurled like a dark tapestry,
Threads of betrayal woven with heartache and pain.
In the swirling mist of the trial, she wandered,
Fragments of her past calling her name.
In the bustling hallway, laughter rang bright,
Yet she felt isolated, a shadow in the crowd.
Friends she thought true turned away from her light,
Their smiles faded, whispers growing loud.
One day, she spotted a group huddled close,
Their joy resonated, but her heart felt a chill.
With hope in her chest, she approached, heart morose,
Yet as she neared, their laughter grew still.
Eyes darted, exchanging glances so cold,
Karen's pulse quickened, a knot in her throat.
With every step closer, the truth began to unfold—
They had shared jokes, her trust turned to smoke.
Then came Ethan, the boy who had captured her heart,
With charm and sweet words, he swept her away.
They whispered their dreams beneath stars, felt the
spark,

But that dream turned to ash with the light of the day.
She recalled the moment her heart broke in two,
In the very spot where their first love ignited.
"Why would you do this?" she asked, voice subdued,
His laughter cut sharp, leaving her slighted.
"It's just a joke, Karen," he said with a smirk,
As if her pain was a game to be played.
Her vulnerability met with a callous quirk,
In that instant, her trust in him frayed.
The memories swirled like shadows around her,
Each one a reminder of the loneliness felt.
The figure of fear loomed, a haunting observer,
Its voice a chilling whisper, the past that had dealt.
"You see? They all abandon you, every last one,
Every time you open your heart, it leads to pain."
The words wrapped around her like a cloak, heavy, done,
She felt the weight of sorrow, drowning in disdain.

18. "I'm here for you"

Karen stood amidst the shadows,
a tempest raging in her heart,
the weight of self-doubt pressing down,
each breath a struggle, each moment heavy.
In the mirror of her mind,
she saw her shadow,
a reflection of pain and shame,
temptation to give up whispering softly,
"Just let go, it's easier this way."
Yet just then, a figure emerged,
Thistle, his presence a beacon,
cutting through the storm,
his voice gentle, yet probing.
"Why can't you let this go?"
Tears brimmed in her eyes,
the storm within swirling fiercely.
"Because this fear holds my pain,"
she whispered,
"memories that linger,
beautiful yet cruel,

haunting me with their illusions,
fake loves that left me empty."
"Is this why you didn't accept Shawn's love?"
he asked, concern woven into his words.
"Yes," she admitted,
the ache deepening in her chest.
"Every time I thought I could open up,
the betrayals rushed back,
the loneliness wrapped around me,
scaring me from the risk."
"Don't you trust me at least?"
Thistle stepped closer,
his gaze unwavering,
"I'm here for you, always."
Her heart twisted,
his words a gentle reminder
of the times he stood by her side,
the comfort of his presence
now overshadowed by fear.
But the figure loomed,
dark and oppressive,
pressing in with her insecurities,
and in that moment,
she resolved to confront it.
"I'm here for you," she whispered,
reaching out toward the shadow,
her fingers brushing its cold surface.

The figure began to shrink,
transforming into a smaller version of herself,
wide-eyed and trembling,
a child lost in the shadows.
The younger self looked up,
tears glistening like stars,
searching for solace in a fractured world.
"Thank you," she whispered,
her voice small and fragile.
Kneeling down,
Karen wrapped her arms around the child,
feeling warmth spread through her heart,
"I'm here now,
you're not alone anymore."
With Thistle by her side,
she embraced her fears,
the parts of herself long hidden,
a journey of healing unfolding,
forgiveness blooming within,
not just for those who had hurt her,
but for herself as well.
This was the moment,
a reclamation of her narrative,
finding strength in vulnerability,
learning to trust again,
as light began to seep
through the cracks of her darkness.

19. Voices united

I stepped out of the mist, feeling light,
The weight of fear lifting,
My heart raced with a single thought—
I had to find him.
Running through the landscape,
Images of my trial fresh in my mind,
Each step fueled by the thought of Thomas,
My guiding light, my strength.
"Karen!" his voice cut through the air,
A rush of relief as I spotted him,
I ran, breathless,
The words poured out,
"You're the reason I passed this trial.
Please, don't leave me."
He gripped my shoulders,
Desperation in his eyes,
"Karen, you are my strength."
In that moment, we embraced,
The warmth of his presence wrapping around me,
An unbreakable shield.

"You're my reason too," I whispered,
Feeling the bond between us,
"You and Thistle mean the world to me."
And as we pulled apart,
I saw the strength mirrored in his gaze,
A silent understanding—
We were no longer alone.
Thistle approached with a proud smile,
"Congratulations on overcoming your fears."
And there stood our mentor,
Calm yet powerful,
"Well done, both of you.
This is the final trial,
But not the end.
Life will continue to challenge you,
Face it together."
We exchanged glances,
Determination coursing through us,
"Thank you," we said,
Voices united.
"Embrace the journey ahead,
You are never truly alone."
With those words in our hearts,
We stepped forward, hand in hand.

20. "I'll always be there for you"

As they walked toward the shimmering portal,
The mentor's presence felt strong yet distant,
Karen's heart weighed heavy,
Thoughts of Thistle swirling in her mind.

"Will she be with us?" she asked,
A tremor in her voice,
The mentor sighed,
"All magical beings belong to this world,
They cannot guide you beyond."

A sadness washed over her,
Tears glistening like morning dew,
She whispered her goodbyes,
Memories of laughter and warmth
Filling the air between them.

Thistle's voice brushed against her ear,
"I'll always be here,

In every whisper of the wind,
In every shadow that dances."

Turning to Shawn,
She saw a spark of hope in his eyes,
"Where is your guide?" she inquired,
Curiosity threading through her heart.

"In the book," he said softly,
"A letter spoke of my guide,
They will be found soon,
Once I enter the enchanted forest."

A smile broke through her sadness,
"Maybe you are my guide in life,"
His words wrapped around her,
A promise of shared journeys ahead.

Together, they stepped toward the portal,
This time calm,
Surrounded by memories,
Visions of their happiest days
Flickering like stars in the night.

The air shimmered with laughter,
Moments captured in time,
As they crossed into the light,

Hearts entwined,

21. A new beginning

As they stepped through the shimmering light,
the enchanted world faded, warmth kissed the night.
"See you tomorrow?" Shawn's voice, soft and clear,
"Definitely," Karen replied, with a smile full of cheer.
Walking home, memories wrapped around her tight,
but Thistle's absence brought shadows to her light.
A thud from the cupboard broke her lingering sigh,
a doll fell to the floor, catching her eye.
It looked just like Thistle, with bright, playful eyes,
a remnant of childhood, where imagination flies.
Realization washed over, joy replaced the pain,
Thistle had never left, she was part of the gain.
Holding the doll close, tears of happiness flowed,
a symbol of dreams, where her spirit had glowed.
From that moment onward, each day felt anew,
with Shawn by her side, together they grew.
Every sunrise a promise, adventures to unfold,
ready to face life, with hearts brave and bold.
Hand in hand, they embraced the wonders of the day,
knowing love was their guide, come what may.

This was just the beginning, the start of their quest,
to explore the world together, feeling truly blessed.
With hope in their hearts, they welcomed tomorrow,
in a journey of laughter, joy, and even sorrow.